US & Israel Relationship
Beneficial or Harmful
S. Parvez

US & Israel Relationship Beneficial or Harmful

The USA funds and Israel

Since 1948, the United States has provided Israel approximately $310 billion in total economic and military assistance, adjusted for inflation. This makes Israel the largest cumulative recipient of U.S. foreign aid.

In addition to government aid, private U.S. funds contribute significantly to Israel, with more than $1.5 billion annually in tax-deductible donations and Israeli bonds. These private contributions, which are separate from the official aid, underscore the depth of the relationship between the two nations, as well as the support from individuals and corporations that align with Israel's economic and security objectives. These financial transfer dynamics are complex and often discussed in the context of geopolitical, economic, and social considerations.

The aid provided by the United States to Israel is primarily used for military purposes. Here are some key ways in which Israel utilizes this aid:

1. Military Equipment and Services: A significant portion of the aid, approximately $3.3 billion annually, is provided through the Foreign Military Financing (FMF) program. These funds are used to purchase U.S. military equipment and services.

2. Missile Defense Systems: A substantial amount is allocated to Israel's missile and rocket defense systems, such as the Iron Dome, David's Sling, and Arrow systems.

3. Advanced Weapons Systems: Funds are also used to acquire advanced weapons systems, enhancing Israel's military capabilities[3].

4. Defense Supplies and Services: Additional aid supports various defense supplies and services, including enhancing weapons production and maintaining military infrastructure.

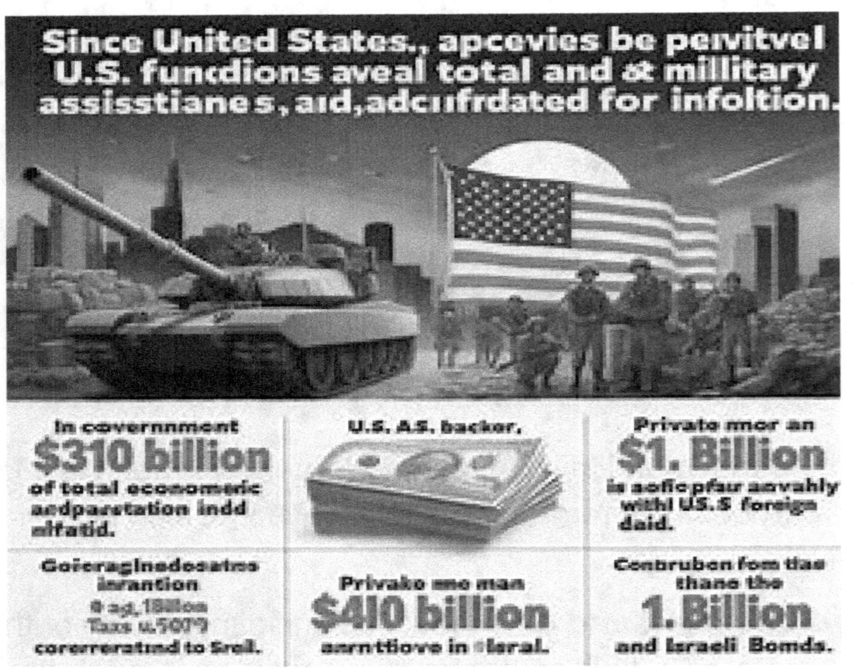

These photographs explain where US tax Money Used

(Will US taxpayers accept responsibility for what is seen in these photographs)

US economic and military assistance to Israel is more than $310 billion. But What Israel has done in Gaza reflects what money is used for. Infants, children, unborn babies, and women have lost lives in thousands. USA, a human rights campaigner could not think of tax money that would be used for this purpose. This is a matter for US taxpayers to think and recently in response protests about the Gaza genocide were done throughout the country.

The U.S. has indeed provided substantial economic and military assistance to Israel, totaling over $310 billion since its founding1. This support has been a cornerstone of U.S. foreign policy, aimed at ensuring Israel's security and maintaining its qualitative military edge in the region.

However, the recent conflict in Gaza has raised significant concerns and sparked widespread protests across the U.S. Many Americans are questioning the use of their tax dollars, especially considering the high civilian casualties reported in Gaza1. The situation has led to a broader debate about U.S. foreign aid and its implications for human rights and international law.

It's a complex and deeply emotional issue, reflecting U.S. society's diverse perspectives and values. How do you feel about the ongoing discussions and protests?

The debate over U.S. aid to Israel is complex, involving considerations of strategic alliances, regional stability, and human rights.

Reevaluating foreign aid policies is a significant step that requires careful consideration of various factors, including national security interests and ethical implications. Citizens need to voice their opinions and engage in discussions about how their tax dollars are used.

The concern about civilian casualties in Gaza is deeply valid and shared by many around the world. The loss of innocent lives, especially among infants, children, and women, is a tragic and heart-wrenching aspect of the conflict.

Addressing this issue involves reconsidering foreign aid and advocating for diplomatic solutions and humanitarian efforts to protect civilians. International pressure and dialogue can be crucial in seeking a peaceful resolution and ensuring that humanitarian laws are respected.

 A thoughtful exploration of how the United States can maintain its global commitments while addressing pressing domestic concerns, such as student debt relief and homelessness.

The interplay of foreign aid, debt forgiveness, and social welfare is a complex and multifaceted issue that reflects the priorities and challenges of a nation. Since 1948, the United States has provided Israel with an estimated $310 billion in economic and military assistance, making it the largest cumulative recipient of U.S. foreign aid. This aid, primarily utilized for military purposes, underscores the strategic partnership between the two nations and the U.S.'s commitment to Israel's security.

However, the issue of homelessness remains a pressing concern, with approximately 653,104 people experiencing homelessness as of January 2023, marking a 12.1% increase from the previous year. The estimated cost to effectively address this crisis is around $20 billion, which would provide permanent supportive housing and essential services to those in need.

The burden of student loans is indeed a significant issue for many individuals, often causing prolonged financial stress. It's important to recognize that there are various programs aimed at alleviating this burden through loan forgiveness and repayment plans. For instance, the Public Service Loan Forgiveness (PSLF) program is designed to forgive the remaining balance on Direct Loans after the borrower has made 120 qualifying monthly payments while working full-time for a qualifying employer. Similarly, the Teacher Loan Forgiveness program offers forgiveness for teachers who work full-time for five complete and consecutive academic years in certain elementary and secondary schools that serve low-income families and meet other qualifications.

Income-Driven Repayment (IDR) plans also offer a route to loan forgiveness after making a certain number of payments over 20 or 25 years, depending on the plan. Additionally, there are specific circumstances under which your federal student loans may be discharged, such as a total and permanent disability discharge, closed school discharge, or borrower defense to repayment if your school misled you or engaged in other misconduct in violation of certain laws.

While these programs provide avenues for relief, the conversation around student loan forgiveness is complex and multifaceted, involving considerations of federal budget priorities, economic policies, and international relations. The allocation of funds to foreign aid, including support to countries like Israel and Ukraine, is part of a broader strategy that encompasses diplomatic, security, and humanitarian objectives. For example, the recent $95 billion foreign aid package passed by the House includes military aid to Ukraine and Israel, replenishing U.S. weapons systems, and providing humanitarian assistance to civilians in Gaza. This aid is seen as an investment in global stability and security, which can have far-reaching impacts, including on the economy.

It's a challenging balance for policymakers to strike, addressing the immediate needs of citizens, such as student loan debt, while also considering long-term international responsibilities and the potential benefits of foreign aid. The debate continues how best to allocate resources to serve both national and international interests effectively. Discussions on student loan forgiveness are ongoing, and it remains a critical topic for many, highlighting the need for solutions that address the financial well-being of individuals while also considering the broader economic and geopolitical landscape.

An essay that weaves these threads into a cohesive narrative could highlight the juxtaposition of international support against domestic needs. It could explore the ethical and economic implications of allocating substantial funds for foreign military aid while significant social issues persist at home. The essay might argue for a balanced approach that does not undermine international obligations but also prioritizes the urgent needs of the nation's most vulnerable citizens. Such a discourse would reflect on past and present policies and prompt a broader conversation on the future direction of U.S. fiscal and social priorities. The main objective would be to examine the allocation of resources in a way that is both globally responsible and domestically equitable, fostering a dialogue on how a nation can navigate its role on the international stage while ensuring the well-being of its people.

The debate surrounding foreign aid is a contentious one, with strong arguments presented on both sides. Proponents of foreign aid argue that it is a moral imperative for wealthier nations to assist less developed countries in their pursuit of economic growth and stability. They contend that foreign aid can lead to improved living standards, bolstered by better healthcare, education, and infrastructure, which in turn can foster global stability and security. Additionally, supporters assert that foreign aid can strengthen diplomatic ties and create economic partnerships that benefit donor countries as well.

On the other hand, critics of foreign aid point to a variety of concerns. They argue that aid can sometimes lead to dependency, undermining the recipient country's incentive to develop sustainable economic policies and industries. There is also the argument that aid can be misused or misallocated, with funds not reaching those in need due to corruption or inefficiency. **Furthermore, skeptics suggest that foreign aid can inadvertently support authoritarian regimes, stifling democracy and human rights in the recipient countries.**

Moreover, some argue that foreign aid can distort local economies, leading to inflation or harming local businesses by flooding markets with donated goods. Others believe that aid can be paternalistic, reflecting the donor's priorities rather than the recipient's needs and that it can perpetuate a cycle of debt and economic instability.

In conclusion, the arguments for foreign aid center on humanitarian assistance, economic development, and the strengthening of strategic alliances, while the arguments against it focus on the risks of dependency, mismanagement, and potential negative impacts on local economies and governance. The challenge lies in designing aid programs that maximize benefits while minimizing potential harms, ensuring that the assistance provided truly supports the long-term development and self-sufficiency of recipient nations. This nuanced understanding of the complexities involved in foreign aid is crucial for informed policy-making and effective international relations.

As of January 2023, there were approximately **653,104 people** experiencing homelessness in the United States[12]. This represents a significant increase of 12.1% from the previous year.

United nation's Resolutions and Results

The United Nations has been a significant platform for international diplomacy and conflict resolution, and its engagement with the Israeli-Palestinian conflict is reflected in numerous resolutions.

Since 1984, the UN has adopted various resolutions addressing the complexities of the conflict, to promote peace, security, and cooperation in the region.

These resolutions have covered many issues, including territorial disputes, human rights concerns, and the broader goal of achieving a two-state solution.

The UN Security Council and the General Assembly have been active in passing resolutions that call for actions from both sides to move toward a peaceful resolution.

It is important to note that the effectiveness of these resolutions often depends on the political will of the member states and the international community to enforce them.

The resolutions serve as a testament to the ongoing efforts of the United Nations to facilitate a peaceful and just solution to the long-standing conflict in the Middle East.

The United Nations has been actively involved in addressing issues related to the Israeli-Palestinian conflict through numerous resolutions.

As of 2013, Israel had been condemned in 45 resolutions by the United Nations Human Rights Council (UNHRC) since its creation in 2006. The UN Security Council (UNSC) adopted 131 resolutions directly addressing the Arab-Israeli conflict from 1967 to 1989.

Additionally, the General Assembly has adopted many resolutions, with 140 resolutions criticizing Israel from 2015 to 2022 alone.

These figures highlight the extensive efforts and attention the United Nations has dedicated to this ongoing conflict.

It's important to note that these resolutions reflect the international community's stance on various aspects of the conflict and are a call for action towards a peaceful resolution.

However, the impact and enforcement of these resolutions depend greatly on the political will and cooperation of member states.

The United Nations General Assembly (UNGA) has passed several key resolutions regarding Israel and the Israeli-Palestinian conflict.

One of the most significant is Resolution 181, passed in 1947, which recommended the partition of Palestine into Arab and Jewish states, with Jerusalem as a corpus separatum under international administration.

Another pivotal resolution is Resolution 194, adopted in 1948, which addresses the status of Jerusalem and the right of return for Palestinian refugees.

More recently, the UNGA demanded that Israel end its 'unlawful presence' in the Occupied Palestinian Territory in a resolution adopted in September 2024, following an advisory opinion by the International Court of Justice.

This resolution calls for Israel to comply with international law, cease all new settlement activity, evacuate settlers, and dismantle parts of the separation wall constructed within the occupied West Bank.

It also emphasizes the need for reparations and the return of displaced Palestinians to their places of origin.

These resolutions, among others, underscore the UNGA's ongoing efforts to address the complexities of the conflict and promote a peaceful resolution.

The effectiveness of these resolutions often hinges on the political will of the member states to enforce them and support the UNGA's decisions.

The United Nations General Assembly (UNGA) and the United Nations Security Council (UNSC) are two distinct bodies within the UN system that serve different purposes with their resolutions.

The UNGA is composed of all United Nations member states and provides a unique forum for multilateral discussion.

It primarily passes resolutions that have a recommendatory nature, meaning they are not legally binding but carry political weight.

These resolutions reflect the international community's opinion and can influence policy and practice.

In contrast, the UNSC is responsible for maintaining international peace and security and can make decisions that member states are obligated to comply with under the United Nations Charter.

When the UNSC passes a resolution, particularly under Chapter VII of the Charter, it can impose sanctions, authorize the use of force, or take other actions deemed necessary to address threats to peace or acts of aggression.

The key difference lies in the resolutions passed by each body. UNGA resolutions, while they can be influential and express the will of the international community, do not have the same enforcement power as those of the UNSC.

The UNSC has a smaller membership, with fifteen members including five permanent members with veto power, which allows it to respond more decisively to international crises.

However, this also means that the actions of the UNSC can be subject to the political interests of its permanent members, which can sometimes lead to inaction in the face of certain conflicts.

In summary, while both the UNGA and UNSC aim to address global issues and conflicts, such as those involving Israel, their resolutions differ in terms of their legal standing and enforceability.

The UNGA's resolutions are broader and more reflective of the international community's stance, whereas the UNSC's resolutions are more focused and carry legal obligations for UN member states.

The effectiveness of these resolutions in addressing conflicts and promoting peace depends on various factors, including the political dynamics within the UN and the international community's commitment to upholding international law and the principles of the United Nations.

The United Nations Security Council (UNSC) has passed numerous resolutions related to Israel, reflecting the body's ongoing engagement with the Israeli-Palestinian conflict. One of the earliest examples is Resolution 242, adopted in 1967 following the Six-Day War, which called for the withdrawal of Israeli armed forces from territories occupied during the conflict and the acknowledgment of the sovereignty, territorial integrity, and political independence of every state in the area.

Another landmark resolution is Resolution 338, passed in 1973, which demanded a ceasefire in the Yom Kippur War and urged the implementation of Resolution 242 in all its parts.

More recently, Resolution 2334, adopted in 2016, stated that Israel's settlement activity constitutes a 'flagrant violation' of international law and has 'no legal validity'.

It demanded that Israel stop such activity and fulfill its obligations as an occupying power under the Fourth Geneva Convention.

In December 2023, a resolution was passed calling for a pause in hostilities and a boost in humanitarian aid for Gaza, highlighting the UNSC's role in addressing the immediate needs of affected populations and calling for actions to support a sustainable cessation of hostilities.

These resolutions are a testament to the UNSC's efforts to mediate the conflict and promote peace.

While the resolutions carry significant international authority, their impact often depends on the political will of the member states to enforce them and the dynamics of international relations.

The UNSC's resolutions related to Israel are part of a broader effort to maintain international peace and security, and they continue to shape the discourse and actions surrounding the Israeli-Palestinian conflict.

The effectiveness of these resolutions in achieving their intended outcomes remains a complex aspect of international diplomacy and conflict resolution.

Israel's responses to United Nations Security Council (UNSC) resolutions have varied over the years, often reflecting the complex political and security considerations at play.

For instance, in response to the recent UNSC resolution calling for a pause in hostilities and increased humanitarian aid for Gaza, Israel's ambassador to the UN stated that the resolution "will have no meaning in practice," asserting that Israel acts according to international law.

This stance indicates a degree of skepticism about the impact of such resolutions, particularly in the context of ongoing conflict and security concerns.

Historically, Israel has at times engaged with the content of UNSC resolutions. In contrast, at other times it has expressed reservations or outright rejection, especially when it perceives the resolutions as one-sided or failing to address its security needs.

For example, after the adoption of Resolution 2334 in 2016, which condemned Israeli settlement activities, Israel rejected the resolution, arguing that it was biased and did not reflect the reality on the ground.

The Israeli government has often emphasized the need for direct negotiations with the Palestinians as the only path to sustainable peace, rather than through international resolutions which it views as counterproductive to the peace process.

The Israeli government's responses are also influenced by internal political dynamics, public opinion, and the international community's reactions.

In some cases, Israel has taken steps to comply with certain aspects of resolutions, particularly those that align with its policy objectives or are under significant international pressure.

However, in many instances, Israel has maintained that security considerations and the need to protect its citizens are paramount, leading to a prioritization of national interests over compliance with UNSC resolutions.

The effectiveness of UNSC resolutions in influencing Israel's policies and actions is a subject of debate.

While these resolutions carry international legal weight, their enforcement often relies on the political will of the international community and the dynamics of global diplomacy.

As such, Israel's responses to UNSC resolutions must be understood within the broader context of the Israeli-Palestinian conflict, regional geopolitics, and the interplay between international law and national sovereignty.

The ongoing dialogue and negotiations, both within the UN framework and in other international forums, continue to shape the discourse and potential pathways toward resolving the conflict.

The international community's view on Israel's responses to United Nations Security Council (UNSC) resolutions is diverse and reflects a spectrum of political stances, strategic interests, and diplomatic priorities.

Many countries, particularly those in the Middle East and members of the Non-Aligned Movement, have historically supported UNSC resolutions critical of Israel's policies, particularly about the occupation and settlement activities in Palestinian territories.

These nations often advocate for strong adherence to international law and express solidarity with the Palestinian cause, urging Israel to comply with UNSC resolutions.

On the other hand, some countries, especially Israel's close allies, may view the resolutions as unbalanced or believe that Israel's security concerns justify certain actions that are otherwise criticized by the international community.

For instance, the United States has frequently used its veto power to block or soften UNSC resolutions that it perceives as unfairly targeting Israel, emphasizing the importance of Israel's right to defend itself and the need for direct negotiations between Israel and the Palestinians.

The European Union and its member states generally support a two-state solution and often endorse UNSC resolutions calling for an end to the occupation and settlement expansion.

However, they also emphasize Israel's security needs and the complexity of the conflict, advocating for a negotiated settlement rather than unilateral actions.

In recent developments, the UN General Assembly voted overwhelmingly to adopt a resolution demanding that Israel end its 'unlawful presence' in the Occupied Palestinian Territory, with a significant majority of nations in favor, indicating a strong international consensus on this issue.

This resolution followed an advisory opinion by the International Court of Justice, which declared Israel's continued presence in the territory as 'unlawful'.

The vote's outcome, with 124 nations in favor, 14 against, and 43 abstentions, showcases the varied perspectives within the international community.

The reactions to Israel's responses to UNSC resolutions can also be influenced by geopolitical shifts, regional alliances, and the evolving nature of international relations.

For example, some Arab states have recently normalized relations with Israel, which may affect their stance on certain resolutions.

Additionally, global powers like China and Russia have their strategic interests in the region and may view Israel's actions through the lens of their broader foreign policy objectives.

Overall, the international community's views on Israel's responses to UNSC resolutions are complex and multifaceted.

While there is a general call for compliance with international law and UNSC decisions, the actual support for these resolutions and the criticism of Israel's responses varies widely among countries, reflecting the intricate web of diplomacy, international law, and the pursuit of peace and security in the region.

The ongoing dialogue and negotiations within the UN framework and other international forums continue to shape the discourse and potential pathways toward resolving the Israeli-Palestinian conflict.

The effectiveness of UNSC resolutions and the international community's response to Israel's actions remain central to the efforts to achieve a lasting and just solution to the conflict.

The Arab League, a regional organization of Arab countries, has historically taken a critical stance towards Israel's responses to United Nations Security Council (UNSC) resolutions.

The League has often echoed the sentiments of its member states, many of which have had longstanding positions in support of the Palestinian cause and have called for Israel to comply with international law and UNSC resolutions.

For instance, the Arab League has supported resolutions like UNSC Resolution 242, which emphasizes the inadmissibility of acquiring territory by war and calls for the withdrawal of Israeli forces from occupied territories.

The Arab League's stance is also reflected in its support for the implementation of UNSC Resolution 2334, which condemned Israeli settlement activities and demanded a halt to such actions.

The League has urged its member states and the international community to ensure the actual implementation of this resolution, demonstrating its commitment to upholding the decisions of the UNSC and advocating for the rights of Palestinians.

In recent years, the Arab League has continued to express its concerns over Israel's policies in Palestinian territories.

During high-level informal interactive dialogues with the Security Council, representatives of the Arab League have called for the acceptance of Palestine's request for full membership at the UN and for the Security Council to assume its responsibilities towards the implementation of relevant resolutions.

This indicates the League's active engagement with the UN to address the Israeli-Palestinian conflict.

Moreover, the Arab League has encouraged its members to align with Security Council resolutions, including those related to youth and women, as part of a broader effort to promote peace, stability, and prosperity in the Arab region.

The League's collaboration with the UN aims to enhance regional capacities in support of the Security Council's mandate and to offer local and regional perspectives on Arab issues on the Council's agenda.

The Secretary-General of the United Nations has acknowledged the cooperation between the UN and the Arab League, particularly in finding a path for the peace process to advance and the occupation to end.

This partnership underscores the League's role in mediating regional conflicts and its influence on international diplomacy concerning the Israeli-Palestinian conflict.

In summary, the Arab League's view of Israel's responses to UNSC resolutions is largely critical and advocates for adherence to international law and the enforcement of UNSC decisions.

The League's actions and statements reflect a collective regional position that seeks to address the rights and aspirations of the Palestinian people and to promote a just and lasting peace in the Middle East.

The effectiveness of the Arab League's stance and its impact on the conflict is intertwined with the dynamics of international relations and the political will of its member states to pursue a unified approach to the Israeli-Palestinian issue.

The ongoing efforts of the Arab League, in cooperation with the UN and other international actors, continue to shape the discourse and potential resolutions to the conflict.

The Arab League remains a key regional player in advocating for the implementation of UNSC resolutions and in seeking a peaceful resolution to the Israeli-Palestinian conflict.

The Organization of Islamic Cooperation (OIC), as a significant regional organization representing Muslim-majority countries, has consistently expressed strong positions on the Israeli-Palestinian conflict, particularly in response to Israel's actions and policies.

The OIC has often condemned Israel's responses to United Nations Security Council (UNSC) resolutions, especially when it perceives those responses as violations of international law and detrimental to the Palestinian cause.

For example, the OIC has characterized some of Israel's actions as "atrocities" and akin to "genocide," reflecting the severity with which the organization views the situation.

This strong language indicates the OIC's support for Palestinian rights and its demand for Israel to adhere to international law and UNSC resolutions.

Furthermore, the OIC has been vocal in its criticism of Israel's treatment of holy sites, particularly in Jerusalem.

The organization has condemned what it sees as aggressive actions by Israeli forces and settlers at the Al-Aqsa Mosque, viewing these as provocations and severe violations of the sanctity of the site, which is revered in Islam.

Such incidents have led the OIC to issue communiqués and hold extraordinary meetings to respond to what it considers infringements on religious rights and freedoms.

The OIC's stance is not only limited to statements of condemnation but also includes calls for action.
The organization has urged the Security Council to enforce its resolutions more effectively and to hold Israel accountable for what the OIC views as violations of international law.

By doing so, the OIC aligns itself with other international voices calling for compliance with UNSC resolutions and the protection of Palestinian rights.

In its interactions with the UN, the OIC has emphasized the importance of the Palestinian cause to its member states and has sought to influence international policy through advocacy and diplomacy.

The organization's commitment to the Palestinian cause is also evident in its support for Palestine's request for full membership at the UN, reflecting its broader goal of achieving recognition and support for Palestinian statehood on the international stage.

The OIC's views and actions are indicative of the broader sentiment among its member states, which often share a collective position on the Israeli-Palestinian conflict.

This shared perspective is rooted in a sense of solidarity with the Palestinian people and a commitment to upholding international law and UNSC resolutions.

The OIC's stance also reflects the organization's role as a voice for the Muslim world in international affairs, particularly on issues that are of profound religious and cultural significance to its members.

Overall, the OIC's view of Israel's responses to UNSC resolutions is one of strong disapproval and concern.

The organization continues to advocate for the rights of Palestinians and the enforcement of international law, using its platform to influence international opinion and policy.

The effectiveness of the OIC's efforts, however, depends on the political dynamics within the organization, the international community's response, and the evolving landscape of Middle Eastern politics.

The OIC remains a key regional player in the ongoing discourse surrounding the Israeli-Palestinian conflict, and its positions are a significant factor in the international community's approach to resolving the issues at hand.

The organization's continued engagement with the UN and its member states highlights the importance of regional organizations in shaping international relations and contributing to the pursuit of peace and justice in global conflicts.

The OIC's perspectives and actions will likely continue to be a part of the international dialogue on the Israeli-Palestinian conflict, as the search for a lasting resolution continues.

The Organization of Islamic Cooperation (OIC) engages in multifaceted collaboration with various regional organizations to address the Israeli-Palestinian conflict, reflecting a commitment to collective action and diplomacy.

The OIC often coordinates with the Arab League, the African Union, and the Non-Aligned Movement, among others, to consolidate positions and advocate for the Palestinian cause on the international stage.

For instance, the OIC has convened extraordinary meetings to discuss urgent developments in the Palestinian territories, particularly in response to actions by Israel that the OIC deems aggressive or in violation of international law.

These meetings serve as platforms for member states to express their views, formulate joint resolutions, and strategize diplomatic efforts to influence international policy.

The OIC also assigns its Secretary-General to communicate with key international stakeholders, including the permanent members of the Security Council and the Secretary-General of the United Nations, to advocate for the enforcement of UNSC resolutions and to seek international protection for the Palestinian people.

This high-level engagement demonstrates the OIC's proactive approach to diplomacy and its efforts to ensure that the voices of its member states are heard in global forums.

Moreover, the OIC collaborates with regional organizations to issue joint communiqués and hold summits that address the Israeli-Palestinian conflict.

These gatherings often result in unified statements condemning what the OIC and its partners view as unlawful Israeli practices and calling for an end to the occupation and the recognition of Palestinian rights.

By presenting a united front, the OIC and its regional allies aim to amplify their message and exert greater influence on the international community.

The OIC's collaboration extends to legal arenas as well, where it participates in international court proceedings to present the collective stance of the Muslim world on the conflict.

The OIC Secretary-General has pleaded before the International Court of Justice, emphasizing the organization's perspective on Israel's policies and practices in the Occupied Palestinian Territory.

This legal advocacy underscores the OIC's commitment to utilizing all available avenues to support the Palestinian cause.

In addition to these diplomatic and legal efforts, the OIC works closely with regional partners to address humanitarian issues arising from the conflict.

The organization calls for the opening of humanitarian corridors and the provision of aid to affected Palestinian populations, coordinating with regional organizations to ensure that assistance reaches those in need.

This humanitarian dimension of the OIC's work highlights the organization's concern for the welfare of civilians impacted by the conflict.

The OIC's collaboration with other regional organizations is not limited to reactive measures in response to specific incidents.

The organization also engages in ongoing dialogue and joint initiatives aimed at long-term conflict resolution and the promotion of peace.

Through regular consultations and collaborative efforts, the OIC and its regional partners seek to maintain momentum in advocating for a just and sustainable solution to the Israeli-Palestinian conflict.

In summary, the OIC's collaboration with other regional organizations is characterized by a combination of diplomatic advocacy, legal action, humanitarian assistance, and strategic partnerships.

This collaborative approach reflects the OIC's role as a key player in regional and international efforts to address the Israeli-Palestinian conflict.

The effectiveness of these efforts is contingent upon the political will of the member states, the receptiveness of the international community, and the evolving dynamics of the conflict.

The OIC's continued engagement with regional organizations and the broader international community is crucial in shaping the discourse and actions surrounding the pursuit of peace and justice in the Middle East.

The organization's multifaceted strategy aims to ensure that the interests and perspectives of the Muslim world are represented and considered in the ongoing efforts to resolve the conflict and achieve lasting peace.

The OIC's collaborative endeavors with regional organizations are an integral part of the international community's collective efforts to address the complex challenges of the Israeli-Palestinian conflict.

The Organization of Islamic Cooperation (OIC) has been actively involved in a variety of joint initiatives with other regional organizations to address issues of common concern, including the Israeli-Palestinian conflict.

One significant collaborative effort is the OIC's partnership with the United Nations High Commissioner for Refugees (UNHCR) to renew the Joint Humanitarian Action Plan (JHAP) for the years 2022-2025.

This plan aims to consolidate the humanitarian strategic partnership and coordination on issues related to internally displaced persons (IDPs) and refugees within the Islamic world.

Another example of the OIC's collaborative efforts is its response to the COVID-19 pandemic.

The OIC launched joint initiatives with its member states and various institutions to promote cooperation and coordination during this global health crisis.

These initiatives were part of a broader joint response to support member states in countering the pandemic's multi-dimensional repercussions and effects.

Furthermore, the OIC has worked closely with the Arab League on resolutions and communiqués, particularly those addressing the Israeli-Palestinian conflict.

For instance, the two organizations have issued joint statements condemning actions perceived as aggressive by Israel and advocating for the rights of Palestinians.

These joint statements often call for an end to the occupation and the recognition of Palestinian rights, reflecting a unified position on the issue.

In terms of economic cooperation, the OIC has been involved in regional projects such as the Trans-Saharan Road (TSR) in

Africa, which is part of its broader efforts to promote regional trade and integration among member countries.

Such initiatives are designed to enhance connectivity and economic development within the Islamic world.

The OIC's engagement with other regional organizations extends to legal advocacy as well.

For example, the OIC Secretary-General has represented the organization's stance before the International Court of Justice, emphasizing the collective perspective of the Muslim world on Israel's policies and practices in the Occupied Palestinian Territory.

These specific joint initiatives highlight the OIC's commitment to leveraging its collective voice and resources in partnership with other regional organizations to address humanitarian, legal, economic, and political issues.The organization's multifaceted strategy underscores the importance of regional cooperation in shaping international relations and advancing the interests of the Muslim world on the international stage.

The OIC's collaborative endeavors with regional organizations are an integral part of the international community's collective efforts to address complex issues such as the Israeli-Palestinian conflict and to promote sustainable development and humanitarian assistance across the Islamic world.

Veto Power

The United States has exercised its veto power in the United Nations Security Council (UNSC) to block resolutions critical of Israel on numerous occasions. This practice has been a significant aspect of the US's foreign policy, reflecting its strategic alliance with Israel.

According to available data, the US has used its veto power at least 53 times since 1972 to veto UNSC resolutions concerning Israel.

This includes vetoes over resolutions addressing various issues such as Israel's military actions, settlement activities in occupied territories, and the broader Arab-Israeli conflict.

The use of the veto power by the US (according to the US) is often seen to protect Israel from what it perceives as one-sided resolutions that do not adequately address the complexities of the conflict or Israel's security concerns.

The frequency of these vetoes highlights the influential role of the US in Middle Eastern geopolitics and its impact on the functioning of the UNSC.

The vetoes have at times led to criticism from other member states and observers who argue that they hinder the ability of the UNSC to fulfill its mandate of maintaining international peace and security.

The US's use of its veto power is also indicative of the broader challenges faced by the UNSC in addressing conflicts where permanent members have strong national interests.

Despite the vetoes, the UNSC continues to be a central forum for international diplomacy and conflict resolution, with its resolutions carrying significant political and moral weight, even when they are not enforced.

The dynamics of the UNSC, including the use of veto power, remain a critical factor in the international community's efforts to address the Israeli-Palestinian conflict and promote peace in the region.

The effectiveness of the UNSC in this regard is contingent upon the political will of its members and the broader international community to support its decisions and work towards their implementation.

The US's vetoes are a testament to the complex interplay between national interests and international diplomacy within the framework of the United Nations.

The ongoing discourse and negotiations within the UNSC and other international forums continue to shape the prospects for resolving the conflict and achieving a lasting peace.

The US's position on UNSC resolutions related to Israel is likely to remain a significant aspect of its foreign policy and a key factor in the international community's approach to the Israeli-Palestinian conflict.

The use of veto power by the US and other permanent members of the UNSC underscores the importance of reforming the Council's decision-making processes to better reflect the realities of contemporary international relations and to enhance its effectiveness in promoting global peace and security.

The US's vetoes also highlight the need for a balanced approach that considers the legitimate security concerns of all parties involved in the conflict while upholding the principles of international law and human rights.

The pursuit of peace in the Middle East continues to be a complex and challenging endeavor, with the actions of the UNSC and its members playing a crucial role in shaping the future of the region.

The US's use of its veto power about UNSC resolutions against Israel remains a subject of debate and analysis, reflecting the intricate balance between diplomacy, national interests, and the quest for peace.

The history of US vetoes in the UNSC is an important aspect of understanding the dynamics of the Israeli-Palestinian conflict and the international community's efforts to address it.

The US's future use of its veto power will continue to be closely watched by observers and stakeholders alike, as it has significant implications for the prospects of peace and stability in the Middle East.

The ongoing efforts to resolve the Israeli-Palestinian conflict and the role of the UNSC in this process underscore the importance of sustained international engagement and the need for a comprehensive approach to conflict resolution that addresses the root causes of the conflict and promotes a just and lasting peace.

The US's vetoes in the UNSC are a reminder of the challenges faced by the international community in navigating the complexities of global politics and the importance of multilateralism in addressing conflicts and promoting peace.

The history of US vetoes against resolutions concerning Israel is a complex tapestry that intertwines with the broader narrative of the Israeli-Palestinian conflict and the international community's response to it.

The US's actions in the UNSC will continue to be a key factor in shaping the international discourse on the conflict and the search for a peaceful resolution.

The effectiveness of the UNSC in addressing the Israeli-Palestinian conflict, and the role of the US's veto power in this context, remain central to the efforts to achieve a lasting and just solution to the conflict.

The pursuit of peace in the Middle East, and the role of the UNSC and the US's veto power in this endeavor, will continue to be a subject of international attention and action in the years to come.

The US's use of its veto power about resolutions against Israel is a significant aspect of the international community's efforts to address the Israeli-Palestinian conflict and will remain an important area of focus for policymakers, diplomats, and observers.

The history of US vetoes in the UNSC is a testament to the enduring complexities of the Israeli-Palestinian conflict and the challenges faced by the international community in seeking to resolve it.

The US's future actions in the UNSC, including its use of veto power, will be closely monitored as they have the potential to significantly influence the course of the conflict and the prospects for peace in the region.

The ongoing dialogue and negotiations within the UNSC and other international forums are crucial for advancing the peace process and achieving a just and sustainable resolution to the Israeli-Palestinian conflict.

The US's vetoes against resolutions concerning Israel reflect the intricate interplay between national interests, international law, and the pursuit of peace, highlighting the need for a concerted and balanced approach to conflict resolution.

The history of US vetoes in the UNSC is an important aspect of the international community's engagement with the Israeli-Palestinian conflict and will continue to shape the discourse and actions surrounding the pursuit of peace in the Middle East.

The US's use of its veto power about resolutions against Israel underscores the challenges and opportunities for international diplomacy and conflict resolution in the context of the Israeli-Palestinian conflict.

The United States has cited various reasons for using its veto power against United Nations Security Council resolutions critical of Israel.

One of the primary reasons is the belief that such resolutions are unfairly biased against Israel and fail to account for the actions of other parties in the conflict.

The US often argues that resolutions should equally address the complexities of the conflict and Israel's security concerns.

For instance, the US vetoed a resolution in 2023 calling for a "humanitarian pause" in the Israel-Hamas war because it did not include respect for Israel's right to defend itself.

This reflects the US stance that Israel, like all nations, has the right to self-defense and that any resolution should recognize this principle.

Additionally, the US has expressed concerns that certain resolutions could undermine direct negotiations between Israel and the Palestinians, which it views as the most viable path to sustainable peace.

The US believes that unilateral actions through the UN may not be conducive to the peace process and that resolutions should support bilateral negotiations without imposing solutions.

This perspective was evident when the US vetoed a resolution in 2011 that would have recognized Palestinian statehood outside of a negotiated agreement with Israel.

Moreover, the US has often emphasized the need for balance in resolutions and has objected to texts that it perceives as one-sided or that do not address the legitimate security concerns of Israel.

The US has argued that resolutions should contribute to peace and stability rather than exacerbating tensions or assigning blame without contributing to a constructive path forward.

The US has a long-standing commitment to Israel's security and often uses its veto to support this ally, especially in instances where it believes Israel is being unfairly targeted.

While the US's use of its veto power has been criticized by some as an impediment to the peace process, the US maintains that its vetoes are in service of a balanced approach to the Israeli-Palestinian conflict and the broader goal of achieving a lasting and just solution.

The reasons cited by the US for its vetoes reflect a multifaceted approach to international diplomacy and conflict resolution.

The US's actions in the Security Council are indicative of the broader challenges faced in achieving consensus on complex international issues and the role of national interests in shaping the decisions of permanent members of the UNSC.

The US's vetoes in the UNSC are a reminder of the challenges faced by the international community in navigating the complexities of global politics and the importance of multilateralism in addressing conflicts and promoting peace.

The history of US vetoes against resolutions concerning Israel is a complex tapestry that intertwines with the broader narrative of the Israeli-Palestinian conflict and the international community's response to it.

The pursuit of peace in the Middle East, and the role of the UNSC and the US's veto power in this endeavor, will continue to be a subject of international attention and action in the years to come.

The international reaction to the United States' vetoes of United Nations Security Council resolutions critical of Israel has been varied and often reflects broader geopolitical alignments and tensions.

Many countries, particularly those in the Middle East and from the Non-Aligned Movement, have expressed frustration and criticism of the US vetoes, viewing them as an impediment to the peace process and a failure to hold all parties accountable to international law.

For instance, after a US veto in 2023, Palestinian officials condemned the action, stating that it made the US "complicit" in war crimes in Gaza.

This sentiment is echoed by various international rights groups and UN officials who have criticized the US for its vetoes, arguing that such actions demonstrate a "callous disregard for civilian suffering" and risk complicity in war crimes.

On the other hand, Israel and its allies often support the US vetoes, arguing that they prevent the passage of resolutions that are seen as one-sided or that fail to recognize Israel's security concerns.

The US has consistently justified its vetoes by stating that the resolutions are imbalanced and do not contribute to the prospects of peace.

For example, the US Deputy Ambassador to the UN stated that a draft resolution calling for a ceasefire was "divorced from reality" and would not advance peace on the ground.

The vetoes have also prompted reactions from rival powers like Russia and China, who have at times used their vetoes to block US-drafted resolutions.

This dynamic illustrates the complex interplay of international diplomacy within the Security Council, where major powers use their veto rights to influence the Council's decisions in line with their national interests and foreign policy objectives.

The European Union and its member states, while generally supportive of a two-state solution and critical of settlement expansion, often emphasize the need for direct negotiations and a balanced approach that considers the security needs of both Israelis and Palestinians.

The EU's response to US vetoes tends to focus on the importance of resuming peace talks and finding a negotiated settlement to the conflict.

The vetoes and the international reactions to them highlight the challenges faced by the Security Council in addressing conflicts where permanent members have strong national interests.

They also underscore the need for reforming the Council's decision-making processes to enhance its effectiveness in promoting global peace and security.

The effectiveness of the Security Council in addressing the Israeli-Palestinian conflict, and the role of the US's veto power in this context, remain central to the efforts to achieve a lasting and just solution to the conflict.

The US's future actions in the Security Council, including its use of veto power, will be closely monitored as they have the potential to significantly influence the course of the conflict and the prospects for peace in the region.

The ongoing efforts to resolve the Israeli-Palestinian conflict and the role of the Security Council in this process underscore the importance of sustained international engagement and the need for a comprehensive approach to conflict resolution that addresses the root causes of the conflict and promotes a just and lasting peace.

Human rights organizations and international legal experts have called for a reassessment of the US's approach, suggesting that it should center on rights and international law.

With increasing discussions around the concept of apartheid about Israeli policies, there is a growing call for the US to reconsider its strategies and prioritize human rights in its mediation efforts.

European Countries

The European response to the Gaza conflict has been mixed, with some countries supporting Israel's right to self-defense and others emphasizing the need for humanitarian considerations and ceasefires.

Supporting Israel:

-Germany and the Czech Republic have been strong supporters of Israel's right to defend itself against attacks. They argue that calls for a ceasefire should not undermine Israel's security.

Calling for Ceasefire and Humanitarian Aid:

Ireland, Belgium, France, Luxembourg, Malta, Portugal, Slovenia, and Spain voted in favor of a UN resolution calling for a ceasefire and humanitarian aid. These countries are concerned about the high civilian casualties and the humanitarian crisis in Gaza.

General EU Stance:

- The European Union has expressed solidarity with Israel while also urging it to consider the humanitarian impact of its military actions[4]. The EU has called for humanitarian corridors and pauses to allow aid to reach those in need.

This division reflects the broader debate within Europe about balancing security concerns with humanitarian responsibilities.

Israel has received substantial financial assistance from both the United States and European countries over the years.

- **Total Aid:** Since its founding, Israel has received about $310 billion in total economic and military assistance from the U.S., adjusted for inflation[1].

- **Recent Aid:** In the past year alone, the U.S. has provided a record $17.9 billion in military aid to Israel[2].

- **European Union (EU):** The EU has provided various forms of financial assistance to Israel, including through the European Neighbourhood Instrument (ENI), which allocated €2 million per annum for cooperation projects from 2014 to 2020.

- Humanitarian Aid: While the EU has also directed significant funds towards humanitarian aid in the region, including support for Palestinians, the exact figures for direct aid to Israel from individual European countries are less centralized and vary by country.

Financial assistance, while intended to support security and stability, can sometimes have unintended consequences, especially in conflict zones.

The humanitarian impact in Gaza, with high civilian casualties and widespread destruction, highlights the need for careful consideration of how aid is used. Ensuring that aid supports peace and humanitarian efforts, rather than exacerbating conflict, is crucial.

Advocating for transparency and accountability in how aid is allocated and used can help address these concerns. Engaging with policymakers, supporting humanitarian organizations, and raising awareness are all ways to contribute to a more balanced and humane approach to foreign aid.

Absolutely, raising awareness and holding policymakers accountable are crucial steps in addressing humanitarian concerns. Here are a few ways you can get involved:

Join Advocacy Groups: Organizations like Amnesty International and Human Rights Watch often campaign for humanitarian issues and can provide platforms for your voice.

Contact Your Representatives: Writing to or meeting with your local representatives can help ensure your concerns are heard at the policy level.

Raise Awareness: Use social media and community events to spread information and engage others in discussions about the humanitarian impact of foreign aid.

Support Humanitarian Efforts: Donating to or volunteering with organizations that provide aid to affected regions can make a direct impact.

Your involvement can make a significant difference.

Collective action can drive significant change. When more people get involved, it amplifies the message and puts greater pressure on policymakers to address humanitarian concerns.

Here are a few more ways to act:

Educational Campaigns: Organize or participate in events that educate others about the humanitarian impact of conflicts and the role of foreign aid.

Petitions: Support or start petitions that call for policy changes or increased transparency in how aid is used.

Media Engagement: Write articles, op-eds, or letters to editors of newspapers and online platforms to raise awareness and share your perspective.

Collective action indeed holds immense power in shaping societal norms and influencing policy decisions. When individuals unite for a common cause, their consolidated efforts can lead to substantial impacts on the community and beyond. This unity often manifests in various forms, such as public demonstrations, petitions, and social media campaigns, each serving as a catalyst for change. The strength of a collective voice can compel policymakers to take notice and act upon pressing humanitarian issues that may otherwise be overlooked. Moreover, collective action fosters a sense of solidarity among participants, reinforcing the belief that every voice matters and that together, they can make a difference. It is a demonstration of democracy in action, where the will of the people is expressed and exercised through peaceful and organized means. The history of social movements has shown that when people come together, they have the power to overturn unjust laws, push for reforms, and hold leaders accountable. In essence, collective action is not just about the immediate changes it can bring but also about the long-term empowerment of individuals and communities to shape their future. It is a testament to the human spirit's resilience and its unwavering pursuit of justice and equity.

Throughout history, there have been numerous instances where collective action has led to significant societal changes. One prominent example is the civil rights movement in the United States during the 1950s and 1960s, which was a pivotal period that saw a series of mass protests leading to legislation that ended legalized racial segregation. Another example is the anti-apartheid movement in South Africa, which combined the efforts of people within the country and international allies to dismantle a system of racial discrimination. More recently, the global environmental movement has seen collective action on an unprecedented scale, with initiatives like Earth Hour and the annual World Cleanup Day mobilizing millions of people worldwide to address climate change and environmental degradation.

In the realm of technology, the open-source software movement is a testament to the power of collective action in the digital age, where developers across the globe collaborate to create and improve software that is freely available to all. The Me Too movement, which gained momentum in 2017, is another example of collective action that has raised awareness about sexual harassment and assault, leading to public discourse and policy changes in various industries. Additionally, the fight for net neutrality has seen internet users and companies come together to advocate for free and open internet access, influencing regulatory decisions and public policy.

These examples demonstrate the diverse ways in which collective action can manifest and the profound impact it can have on society. Whether it's through peaceful protests, social media campaigns, or collaborative projects, when people unite with a shared vision, they have the power to enact change and address the challenges facing their communities and the world at large. Collective action remains a powerful tool for social progress and a reflection of the human capacity for cooperation and solidarity.

Sustaining momentum in collective movements is a multifaceted endeavor that requires strategic planning and continuous engagement. It involves maintaining the energy, engagement, and support over time, which is crucial for the longevity and impact of any movement. One of the key strategies is the continuous recruitment of new members to keep energy levels high and diversify perspectives within the group. Effective communication strategies are also vital, ensuring that the group's message remains relevant and compelling. Adapting to demographic changes is important, as shifts in the population can impact the priorities and methods of social movements. Utilizing social media platforms can help maintain engagement by providing tools for quick updates, organizing events, and sharing successes. Celebrating milestones and victories can boost morale and reaffirm commitment among supporters.

Research suggests that the most effective campaigns start small and turn local connections into larger networks through organization and social influence. A shared concern among supporters for a particular issue, coupled with an urgency to make change, is where movements begin. Consumer psychology recognizes the power of social influence where one person can impact another person's beliefs and behaviors. Successful movements connect people with the cause, and to one another, before assembling a network to expand their reach.

The experience of participating in collective action can foster continued commitment to a cause. Gaining broader support from society is key to the success of social movements, and the nature of collective action employed can mobilize support or elicit backlash from the general public. Solidarity is seen as transformative strategies and practices that nurture interdependent relationships, building collective power essential for the thriving of movements.

In conclusion, sustaining momentum in collective movements is about strategically managing resources, fostering community connections, and adapting to changing circumstances. It's about ensuring that the goals of the movement remain in public consciousness and are actively pursued. By continuously mobilizing resources and fostering connections within communities, movements can build lasting advocacy efforts that push their agendas forward and influence policymakers to draw attention to their causes.

Historical examples of sustained collective movements are numerous and highlight the enduring power of collective action. The abolitionist movement, which spanned several decades, was instrumental in ending slavery and was characterized by persistent activism, literature, and political lobbying. The labor movement, particularly in the late 19th and early 20th centuries, brought about significant changes in workers' rights through strikes and unionizing efforts. The suffrage movement, which fought for women's right to vote, is another example of a sustained collective movement that, despite facing considerable opposition, eventually succeeded in many countries around the world.

The civil rights movement in the United States, led by figures such as Martin Luther King Jr., is a prime example of a sustained movement that used nonviolent protest to challenge and eventually dismantle institutionalized racial segregation and discrimination. Similarly, the anti-apartheid movement in South Africa, which included both domestic and international efforts, played a crucial role in ending the system of apartheid and establishing majority rule.

Environmental movements have also demonstrated sustainability, with ongoing efforts to address climate change, pollution, and conservation. The conservationist movement, for example, has a long history of advocating for the preservation of natural habitats and biodiversity. The modern environmental movement, which began in the 1950s, has been sustained through public awareness campaigns, policy advocacy, and international agreements on environmental protection.

The LGBTQ+ rights movement has seen sustained efforts to achieve equality and acceptance, with significant legal and social advancements made over the years. This movement has utilized a variety of tactics, from legal challenges to pride parades, to advocate for the rights of LGBTQ+ individuals.

In the digital age, the open-source software movement has shown how sustained collective action can occur in the realm of technology, with developers around the world collaborating to create and maintain free software available to all. This movement has been sustained through a shared ethos of collaboration and innovation.

These movements, among others, demonstrate the potential for sustained collective action to bring about long-term social, political, and environmental change. They show that with perseverance, organization, and a clear vision, collective movements can maintain momentum and achieve their goals, often transforming societies in profound ways. The success of these movements lies in their ability to adapt to changing circumstances, engage new participants, and remain focused on their objectives over time. They serve as powerful reminders of the capacity for collective action to shape history and drive progress.

Fall of a Powerful Kingdom

In the heart of a vast empire, where the sun kissed the golden spires of a thousand temples, there reigned a King whose dominion stretched as far as the eye could see. This sovereign, revered and feared in equal measure, was not just the custodian of a great dynasty but also a father. His son, the apple of his eye, was raised amidst unparalleled opulence and the unyielding echo of 'yes' that resonated through the marble halls of the palace. As the prince matured, so did his whims, and with each passing day, his desires grew more capricious, his demands more extravagant.

Yet, it was not the lavishness that shadowed his steps that defined him, but a burgeoning arrogance that soon became his most faithful companion. The prince, now a mirror of hubris, found a cruel pleasure in the suffering of others, his heart untouched by the cries that rose from the very souls he tormented. The small, sovereign states that dotted the periphery of the empire, though independent, lay under the heavy gaze of the kingdom. It was into these lands that Prince Yahu, with the might of an army that could eclipse the sun, would march. His incursions were not for land or gold, but for the twisted joy of subjugation, leaving behind a trail of anguish and desolation.

Complaints of the prince's brutality climbed like ivy up the walls of the palace, only to fall on deaf ears. The King, ensnared by paternal love, turned a blind eye to the atrocities committed, his silence a thunderous affirmation of the prince's actions. In doing so, the King not only ignored the pleas of his beleaguered neighbors but also sowed the seeds of fear and resentment, a dark harvest that would one day seek the light. Thus, the dynasty that stood unchallenged for ages now teetered, imperceptibly, on the precipice of ruin, its fate intertwined with the caprices of a prince who knew no bounds and a King who knew no 'no'.

As the days turned to months, and months to years, the empire, once a beacon of prosperity and justice, began to crumble from within. The prince, now known as Yahu the Tyrant, had woven a tapestry of terror that blanketed the neighboring states. His deeds, dark as the night, were whispered in hushed tones across the land, for fear that even speaking of them would invoke his wrath. The King, once a just ruler, had become a mere shadow, his legacy tarnished by the actions of his only son.

The states under the yoke of the empire, their patience worn thin by years of suffering, started to forge secret alliances. They knew that to challenge the prince openly would be to invite destruction upon themselves. Instead, they chose to bide their time, waiting for the perfect moment to strike. In the cover of darkness, messengers flitted between these states, carrying with them the hope of a future free from the prince's cruelty.

Meanwhile, in the heart of the empire, whispers of discontent began to stir among the people. The prince's arrogance had not only brought misery to the neighboring lands but had also seeped into the lives of his own subjects. The markets, once bustling with trade, now stood silent, the artisans and merchants fearful of the prince's capricious taxes and laws. The fields lay barren, for the farmers refused to toil when their labor only fed the prince's lavish feasts.

In the palace, the King's advisors, once silent, now spoke in urgent tones. They saw the writing on the wall; the empire could not sustain itself if the prince's tyranny continued unchecked. They implored the King to act, to curb his son's excesses before it was too late. But the King, blinded by love and pride, dismissed their concerns, believing his dynasty unassailable, his rule divine.

The tension between the empire and its neighbors grew taut like a bowstring. Incidents at the borders became more frequent, and the prince's incursions more daring. It was only a matter of time before the bowstring snapped. And when it did, it was not with a single, momentous event, but with a series of small, seemingly inconsequential acts of defiance that the end began.

A farmer refusing to pay tribute, a merchant hiding his goods, a soldier deserting his post – these acts of rebellion, small ripples in the vast ocean of the empire, began to converge into a wave. This wave, powered by the collective will of a people yearning for change, grew in strength and size until it could no longer be ignored.

The first true test came when a small state, emboldened by the growing unrest, openly defied the prince. Yahu, in his fury, mustered his army and marched forth to crush the rebellion. But as he arrived at the borders, he found not a meek and cowering populace, but a united front of soldiers and citizens alike, ready to defend their home.

The battle that ensued was unlike any the empire had seen. The prince's army, though formidable, was met with a resistance fueled by years of pent-up anger and desperation. The fighting was fierce, and the losses heavy on both sides, but the tide had turned. The small state's defiance served as a beacon, igniting the flames of rebellion across the empire.

One by one, the states rose, their alliances coming to light, their armies marching in unison against the prince's forces. The empire, so long unchallenged, found itself besieged on all fronts. The King, finally realizing the gravity of the situation, attempted to stem the tide, but it was too late. The bonds of fear and oppression that had held the empire together were breaking, and with them, the dynasty's grip on power.

The fall of the empire was not a swift one; it was a slow, agonizing unraveling of a tapestry woven over centuries. The prince, his army dwindling, his allies few, fought with the ferocity of a cornered beast. But the more he fought, the more he lost, and with each defeat, his arrogance gave way to desperation.

In the end, it was not a grand battle that sealed the fate of the prince and his empire, but a quiet surrender. The states, now free from the prince's tyranny, formed a new alliance, one based on mutual respect and cooperation. The King, his eyes finally open to the destruction wrought by his son, abdicated his throne, leaving the empire to reckon with the aftermath of his rule.

The tale of the empire and its fall became a cautionary one, told across the lands for generations to come. It served as a reminder that no dynasty is invincible, that the actions of a single individual can alter the course of history, and that the power held by any ruler is not absolute but granted by the will of the governed. And so, the once-great empire passed into legend, its rise and fall a testament to the enduring spirit of the people and the fleeting nature of power.

In the aftermath of the empire's dissolution, Prince Yahu found himself a pariah, stripped of his power and his army. The once-feared tyrant was now a fugitive in his own land, fleeing from the very people he had once subjugated. His name, which had echoed with dread throughout the halls of power, was now spat out as a curse by those who had suffered under his rule.

As the new alliance of states began to rebuild from the ruins, they sought justice for the prince's countless transgressions. Bounty hunters and soldiers of fortune roamed the countryside, eager to capture the disgraced prince for the substantial reward offered. Yet, Yahu proved elusive, using his intimate knowledge of the empire's landscape to evade capture time and again.

The prince's fall from grace was as steep as his rise to infamy had been. With each passing day, his situation grew more desperate. Gone were the luxuries and the sycophants that had surrounded him; in their place were the harsh realities of survival and the relentless pursuit of his enemies. His arrogance, once as unyielding as the stone walls of the palace, began to crack, revealing a man unprepared for a life of hardship.

Rumors of his sightings spread like wildfire, each more fantastical than the last. Some claimed he had taken refuge in the mountains, living as a hermit among the crags and peaks. Others whispered that he had been seen in the bustling marketplaces of distant lands, his royal visage hidden beneath the garb of a commoner. But these were just stories, the truth of his fate as elusive as the man himself.

As months turned into years, the legend of Prince Yahu grew. He became a specter, a cautionary tale told to unruly children, a symbol of the perils of unchecked power and pride. The new rulers of the alliance made it clear that the era of tyranny was over, and that justice would be the cornerstone of their governance. They worked tirelessly to heal the wounds of the past, to forge a future where no single individual could hold such sway over the fate of many.

The prince's legacy, however, lived on in the collective memory of
the empire. It served as a stark reminder of the darkness that can
arise when love and duty are blinded by absolute power. The
King, in his final days, lamented the path his son had taken, his
heart heavy with the knowledge that his own indulgence had
played a part in the empire's fall.

In the end, the fate of Prince Yahu remained shrouded in mystery.
Some say he perished in the wilderness, alone and forgotten.
Others believe he found redemption in a life of anonymity; his
deeds of cruelty were replaced by acts of penance. But the truth
of what became of the prince is known only to the winds of time,
which carry with them the tales of empires and the echoes of
those who once walked their hallowed grounds. What is certain is
that the prince's story is a testament to the enduring human spirit
and the relentless pursuit of justice, a narrative that will continue
to resonate through the ages.

Upon his abdication, the King was swept into the silent eddies of
history, his reign a mere whisper in the grand tapestry of the
empire's legacy. Stripped of his crown and the loyalty of his
subjects, he retreated into the shadows of the world he once ruled
with an iron fist. The palace, with its echoing halls and towering
columns, no longer welcomed him, for it stood as a monument to
his failures as much as to his once-great power.

The King, now a figurehead without a throne, sought solace in solitude. He wandered the lands he had governed, a solitary traveler cloaked in the remnants of his past glory. His journey was one of reflection, a quest for atonement for the suffering his blindness had wrought upon his people and the neighboring states. The weight of his son's tyranny, the cries of the oppressed, the fires of rebellion—all bore heavily upon his conscience.

In his exile, the King came to understand the true cost of his indulgence. The love he bore for his son, once pure and unyielding, had become a poison that seeped through the veins of his dynasty, corrupting the roots of his lineage. He realized that his silence had been as destructive as the prince's actions, a silent consent that had allowed darkness to flourish.

The former monarch found himself in villages and towns, places where his name was spoken with a mixture of reverence and resentment. He listened to the stories of his subjects, tales of hardship and endurance, of lives upended by the whims of a prince they had never chosen. In these stories, the King found the seeds of redemption, not for his name, but for his soul.

He spent his remaining years in humble service to those he had once ruled over. With hands that had once held a scepter, he now offered aid to the needy, comfort to the sorrowful, and apologies to the wronged. His presence became a balm to some, a reminder of a painful past to others, but always, it was a testament to his desire to make amends.

The King's legacy, once destined to be etched in stone and gold, was now written in the hearts of those he served. He became a symbol of the fallibility of power, a cautionary tale of the perils of unchecked authority. His story was told alongside that of the empire, a dual narrative of rise and fall, of glory and ruin.

As the years passed, the King's health waned, and with it, his ability to wander the lands. He settled in a small, unassuming village on the outskirts of the empire he once called his own. There, he lived out his days in a modest dwelling, far removed from the opulence of his former life. The villagers, who had once feared the mention of his name, now offered him the respect due to an elder, recognizing not the King he had been, but the man he had become.

In the quiet twilight of his life, the King found a measure of peace. He passed away not on a throne, but on a simple bed, surrounded by those who had come to know him not as a ruler, but as a man. His passing was marked not by the fanfare of royalty, but by the genuine grief of those who had come to appreciate the quiet, steadfast presence he had offered in his final years.

The King's death was a quiet affair, and he was laid to rest in a grave marked not by grandeur, but by simplicity. A stone, carved with neither his name nor his title, stood at the head of his resting place—a symbol of his final wish to be remembered not as a King, but as a man who had learned the hard lessons of life.

And so, the King's story ended, not with the clamor of battle or the splendor of the court, but with the whisper of leaves in the wind and the soft murmur of a world moving forward. His tale, intertwined with that of the empire and the prince, would live on, a narrative of human frailty, of power and its consequences, and of the enduring quest for redemption that defines the human spirit.

In the wake of Prince Yahu's fall, the neighboring states found themselves at the dawn of a new era. The oppressive shadow that had loomed over them for so long had been lifted, giving way to a light of hope and the promise of a fresh start. These states, once fragmented by fear and subdued by the might of Yahu's army, began to weave a tapestry of unity and resilience.

Leaders from each state convened, their meetings marked by a spirit of collaboration that had been absent for generations. They shared tales of their sufferings and their triumphs, finding common ground in their mutual desire for peace and prosperity. The bonds forged in the crucible of Yahu's tyranny now served as the foundation for a robust alliance, one built on mutual respect and shared goals.

The states worked diligently to repair the damage inflicted upon their lands and people. Villages that had been razed were rebuilt, not just as they were, but better, with stronger structures and a renewed sense of community. Markets that had once been stifled by the prince's greed now thrived, as trade routes reopened and merchants from distant lands brought goods and wealth to their ports.

A collective council was established, with representatives from each state, to ensure that the voices of all were heard and that no single power could dominate. This council became a beacon of democratic governance, a stark contrast to the autocratic rule that had once overshadowed the region. Laws were enacted to protect the rights of the citizens, to ensure fair treatment and to prevent the rise of another tyrant.

Education and knowledge, which had been tools of the elite under Yahu's rule, were now democratized. Schools and libraries were constructed, and scholars from across the land were invited to teach and learn. The exchange of ideas and the pursuit of knowledge became valued pillars of society, fostering innovation and progress.

The military forces of the states, once used for suppression and conquest, were transformed into guardians of peace. Soldiers were retrained to serve and protect, and the armies were united under a single banner of defense. This new military alliance stood not for aggression, but for the protection of the freedom they had all fought so hard to achieve.

Culturally, the states experienced a renaissance. Artists, musicians, and poets, who had once been silenced by the prince's cruelty, now found their voices. The arts flourished, and with them, the cultural identities of each state were celebrated and preserved. Festivals and gatherings became common, with people from different states coming together to share in their diverse heritage.

The environment, too, saw a revival. The lands, which had been neglected and exploited, were nurtured back to health. Forests were replanted, rivers cleansed, and wildlife protected. The states recognized that their natural resources were not just commodities to be used, but treasures to be safeguarded for future generations.

As for the political landscape, the states maintained their sovereignty, but they did so with a newfound understanding of interdependence. They knew that their fates were intertwined, and that cooperation was the key to maintaining their freedom and security. Diplomacy and dialogue replaced intimidation and conflict, and the region became a model of international relations.

The legacy of Yahu's tyranny served as a constant reminder of what could happen when power was left unchecked. It was a lesson that was not forgotten, and it guided the leaders and citizens alike in their decisions and actions. The neighboring states, once under the thumb of a despot, had emerged not just unbroken, but stronger and more united than ever before.

In time, the region once dominated by the empire became known for its stability and its commitment to the welfare of its people. The neighboring states, through their collective efforts, had transformed their shared history of oppression into a future of opportunity and hope. They stood together, a testament to the power of unity and the enduring human spirit, a shining example of what can be achieved when people come together for the greater good. The fall of Yahu was not the end of their story, but the beginning of a new chapter, one filled with promise and potential for generations to come.

The remnants of Yahu's once formidable army, scattered and leaderless after his fall, faced a future fraught with uncertainty. The soldiers, who had marched under the prince's banner, now found themselves without purpose or direction. Many, disillusioned by the prince's tyranny and the subsequent collapse of the empire, chose to lay down their arms and return to the lives they had left behind. They sought to reintegrate into the societies they had once oppressed, hoping for forgiveness and a chance to start anew.

Some of the soldiers, unable to shake off the discipline and camaraderie of military life, banded together to form mercenary groups. They sold their services to the highest bidder, their skills in warfare becoming their only currency in a world that had moved on from the empire's dominion. These mercenaries roamed the lands, their loyalty tied not to a flag or a cause, but to the promise of gold and the survival of their brotherhood.

Yet, there were those among Yahu's army who could not accept the end of the empire. These loyalists, still clinging to the vestiges of their former glory, became outlaws and bandits. They preyed upon the vulnerable, raiding villages and caravans, a constant reminder of the chaos that had once reigned. Their actions posed a significant challenge to the newly established order, prompting the alliance of states to take decisive action against them.

The alliance, determined to maintain the hard-won peace, dispatched their unified forces to hunt down the remnants of the prince's army. Skirmishes broke out in the hinterlands, as the alliance's troops sought to dismantle the last pockets of resistance. These confrontations were often brutal, a stark contrast to the spirit of reconciliation that the alliance was trying to foster.

In time, the efforts of the alliance began to bear fruit. The bandit groups were gradually disbanded, their members captured or forced into hiding. The mercenaries, seeing the changing tides, began to disperse, their unity fraying as the demand for their services dwindled. The soldiers who had returned to civilian life worked hard to prove their worth, their contributions to the rebuilding efforts helping to mend the fabric of society.

As the years passed, the memory of Yahu's army faded into the annals of history. The soldiers who had once marched under the prince's command became farmers, craftsmen, and traders. Their legacy, once defined by conquest and subjugation, was now rewritten by the peace and stability they helped to uphold in their new roles.

The alliance of states, ever vigilant, established a system of watchtowers and patrols to safeguard their borders. They recognized that the security of their lands depended not just on the strength of their armies, but on the prosperity and happiness of their people. Investments were made in infrastructure and education, ensuring that the allure of the sword would be overshadowed by the promise of a pen.

In the end, the remnants of Yahu's army were absorbed into the tapestry of the region's history. Their story, a complex wave of valor and vice, served as a lesson for future generations. It was a reminder that the might of an army is not measured solely by its capacity for war but by its ability to adapt and find purpose in a world that seeks peace above all else. The soldiers of a fallen prince, once instruments of tyranny, had become the architects of their own redemption, their fates a testament to the enduring human capacity for change and growth.

The pivotal moment of defection came during the twilight of Yahu's reign, as the tides of fortune were turning against the once invincible empire. General Arman, a seasoned warrior who had risen through the ranks to become one of Yahu's most trusted commanders, found himself at a crossroads. He had witnessed the prince's descent into tyranny, the needless suffering of the people, and the growing unrest that rippled through the empire. His heart, once loyal to the crown, now harbored doubts that grew heavier with each passing day.

It was on the eve of what was to be a decisive battle, a show of force meant to quell the burgeoning rebellion, that General Arman's resolve crystallized. The camp was alive with the din of preparation, the air thick with anticipation. But amidst the clamor, Arman sought solitude, wrestling with the knowledge that the path he was on led only to further bloodshed and sorrow.

As he walked among the tents, the general's gaze fell upon the soldiers under his command. They were young, many no more than boys, their faces etched with a determination that belied their fear. These were the sons of the empire, and in their eyes, Arman saw the reflection of his own son, who had perished not in battle, but at the hands of the prince's cruelty.

The weight of this realization was a burden too great to bear. Arman understood that his allegiance to Yahu was not just a betrayal of the neighboring states, but a betrayal of his own people, his own family. The general knew that the coming dawn would bring with it a choice that would define not just his fate, but the fate of the empire itself.

Under the cloak of night, General Arman made his decision. He penned a letter, a missive that laid bare his intentions and his heart. With a heavy soul, he entrusted the letter to his most loyal aide, instructing him to deliver it to the leaders of the alliance. In it, he offered his knowledge, his sword, and his loyalty, not to a prince or a kingdom, but to the cause of peace and the future of the lands he called home.

As the first light of morning broke the horizon, General Arman donned his armor for the last time. He addressed his troops, his voice steady, his words imbued with a finality that resonated in the silent air. He spoke not of conquest, but of honor, not of obedience, but of choice. And with a solemn vow to stand for what was just, he led his men not into battle, but away from it, towards the alliance and a new dawn.

The defection of General Arman was a blow from which Yahu's forces would never recover. It was a signal to the empire and the neighboring states alike that the winds of change were upon them. Arman's act of defiance was the spark that ignited the flames of rebellion, inspiring others within Yahu's ranks to question their oaths and their purpose.

The alliance welcomed Arman and his men with a guarded optimism. The general's knowledge of Yahu's strategies and fortifications proved invaluable, and his leadership bolstered the morale of the allied forces. Together, they fortified their positions, preparing for the inevitable backlash that would come with the prince's realization of the betrayal.

When news of Arman's defection reached the palace, it was met with a fury that shook the very foundations of the empire. Yahu, enraged by the perceived treachery, vowed retribution. But his threats were the cries of a desperate man, his authority crumbling like the walls of his besieged empire.

The battle lines were redrawn, and the alliance, now strengthened by the addition of Arman's forces, stood united against the prince. The ensuing battles were fierce, but the momentum had shifted. The alliance, once on the defensive, now took the fight to Yahu's doorstep, their cause emboldened by the general's defection.

General Arman's choice to defeat was not just a military maneuver; it was a statement, a declaration that the time of tyrants was over. His courage became a beacon for all who yearned for freedom, his name synonymous with the virtues of honor and integrity.

The general's legacy was not one of conquest but of liberation. His defection marked the turning point in the struggle against Yahu's tyranny, a moment in history that would be recounted for generations as the beginning of the end for an empire that had lost its way. It was a testament to the power of conscience over obedience, of justice over oppression, and of hope over fear.

General Arman's letter to the alliance, penned under the shroud of night and heavy with the gravity of his decision, was a missive of both confession and commitment. It began with an acknowledgment of his role in the empire's campaigns, expressing a deep remorse for the pain and suffering inflicted upon the neighboring states. He wrote of the countless nights haunted by the cries of the innocent, and the realization that loyalty to a tyrant was complicity in tyranny.

He continued by renouncing his allegiance to Prince Yahu, declaring that his eyes had been opened to the true nature of the prince's rule — one not of strength and prosperity, but of fear and oppression. Arman spoke of his son, whose life had been cut short not by the hazards of war, but by the cruelty of the prince's regime. This personal loss, he confessed, was the catalyst for his change of heart, transforming his unwavering loyalty into a resolute defiance.

The general then offered his knowledge of the empire's military strategies, fortifications, and weaknesses. He provided detailed accounts of the prince's tactics, the disposition of his forces, and the locations of supply caches and strategic strongholds. Arman assured the alliance of his commitment to their cause, pledging to serve not as a general of an oppressive army, but as a soldier in the fight for freedom and justice.

He implored the leaders of the alliance to consider his offer, not out of a desire for redemption or reward, but for the sake of the countless lives that could be spared from further conflict. Arman emphasized that his defection was not a mere shift in loyalty, but a heartfelt desire to prevent further bloodshed and to contribute to the establishment of a lasting peace.

The letter concluded with a solemn vow. General Arman swore to uphold the values of honor and integrity, to protect the innocent, and to stand against tyranny in all its forms. He acknowledged that trust must be earned, and he was prepared to prove his intentions through actions, not just words.

In his closing words, Arman expressed hope that his defection would serve as a turning point in the conflict, a moment when the cycle of violence could be broken, and a new chapter of collaboration and unity could begin. He sealed the letter with his seal, a symbol of his former status, now repurposed as a token of his new allegiance.

The letter, once delivered, resonated deeply with the leaders of the alliance. It was a testament to the power of conscience and the possibility of change, even among those who had once been enemies. General Arman's words became a beacon of hope, inspiring others within the empire to question their loyalties and to consider the legacy they wished to leave behind. It was a pivotal moment in the history of the region, one that will be remembered as the first step toward a future defined by peace rather than conquest.

About the Author

Sarwat Parvez each book in the series seems to cater to different interests, from the fantastical to the factual, the mysterious to the spiritual, and the emotional to the educational. This diversity showcases the author's versatility and offers many readers a rich tapestry of content. Whether seeking escapism, knowledge, or an emotional rollercoaster, this series appears to have something for everyone.

The summaries provided here are based on the titles and themes inferred from the user's message, aiming to glimpse the potential scope and content of the series. So far, he has published 67 books.

1.   The World of Fiction and Imagination Part 1. Stories (The World of Fictions and Imagination)
2.   Haunted World Series:
3.   The Haunted World Series 2. Afghanistan Kindle Edition.
4.   Haunted World Series 3. Albania Kindle Edition.
5.   Struggling Life and Love (Love and Hate) Kindle Edition.
6.   The Old Young Man (Love and Hate Book 2).
7.   World of Spying Series. 1. Arms Dealer. 2. Hidden Past.
8.   Love and Hate.
9.   Angles From Heaven To Earth.
10.   The World of Fiction and Imagination Series. 2. Eleven Stories (The World of Fictions and Imagination).
11.   Sheriff Walter Simson Suspense Series.
12.   Morphological Guide of Human and Animal Pathogenic Fungi & Medical Mycology Lab Manual.
13.   Mysterious Mysteries of the World.
14.   Can humans write a Quraan?
15.   Love and Hate Series 2. Betrayal and Love (Hate and Love).
16.   Love Suspense (Hate and Love).
17.   Haunted India Series 1. Haunted Delhi & Kashmir
18.   Kingdom of Love (Love and Hate)
19.   Islamic Series 3. Sufism V Hinduism (The Origin and Spread of Islam)
20.   Research Trends in Medical Sciences Series
21.   The Horror States of America Series (Haunted Places and Horror Stories of USA Series Book 1)
22.   The Horror States of America Series 2: Arizona (Haunted Places and Horror Stories of USA Series)
23.   Horror States of America Series 3. Arkansas (Haunted Places and Horror Stories of USA Series)
24.   Horror States of America Series 4. California (Haunted Places and Horror Stories of USA Series)
25.   Haunted States of America 5. Maryland The America in Miniature (Haunted Places and Horror Stories of USA Series)
26.   Songs-Poetry for Singers and Movies (Songs-Poetry-Ghazals-Nazm-Gane-Kavita)
27.   Molecular Diagnosis of Fungal
34. Vanishing of Buddhism From India
35. The Changing World From 10,000 BCE-2024 AD36. The Unsung Heroes of the USA
37. Hidden Gems of the World (Beautiful World)
38. Religions of the World Other Than Islam, Christianity, Hinduism, Judaism and Buddhism
39. Summer Wonders of the World (Beautiful World)40. Stories of Teenagers
41. Face, Scalp, Nails, and Skin Diseases. Whether you have or not, check here. Part 1. Human Face Infections (Medical Publications)
42. Face, Scalp, Nails, and Skin Diseases. Whether you have or not, check here Part 2. Human Nail Diseases (Medical Publications)
43. Mysteries of Amazon Forest Stories (Mysterious Mysteries)
44. Ada's Luminarium: The Ethereal Engine Chronicles (The World of Fictions and Imagination)
45. Eerie, and Love Stories About Historical Forts of the USA (Forts of USA)
46. The Bonds We Build: Stories of Enduring Companionship (The World of Fictions and Imagination)
47. "Echoes of Valor" Chronicles of the Great War Based on Real Stories of WW1
48. "Echoes of Faith: A Journey Through Islamic History"
49. Way to Heaven Part 1 (Way to Heaven: The Qur'an)
50. Way To Heaven Part 2
51. Way To Heaven Part 3 (Way to Heaven: The Qur'an)
52. Way to Heaven Part 4
53. Angels Fell on Earth Part 2
54. The Untold Stories of The Himalayas
55. Angles Fell on Earth Part 1
56. Sherif Walter Simson Series "Echoes of the Unseen: The Simson Paradox"
57. What Happened When
59. Medical Mycology Second Edition
60. "Resonance of Emotions: The Universal Symphony": Songs and Poetry
61. Stories of Billionaires: Determination & Courage
62. Drama Series 1. Three Dramas
63. Mysterious Empty Desert of Saudi Arabia
64. Stories of the Sahara Desert
65. Haunted World Stories Revised

All these books are available on Amazon

84

Diseases From Clinical Samples & Medical Mycology Lab Manual (Research Trends in Medical Sciences) 28. Love Stories (Hate and Love) 29. Top 20 Muslim Soccer Players of the World (World of Sports) 30. Postmortem of Democracy (World Politics) 31. दलि की सदायें, नगमाती सरग़ोशियाँ (Songs-Poetry-Ghazals-Nazm-Gane-Kavita) 32. The Life of Journalists 33. USA Presidential Election System	

www.ingramcontent.com/pod-product-compliance
Lightning Source LLC
Chambersburg PA
CBHW061513250726
48657CB00005B/1838